PHILOSOPHERS OF THE SPIRIT

RUMI

PHILOSOPHERS OF THE SPIRIT

RUMI

Edited by
Robert Van de Weyer

Hodder & Stoughton
LONDON SYDNEY AUCKLAND

British Library Cataloguing in Publication Data:
A record for this book is available from the British Library.

ISBN 0 340 69468 8

Typeset in Monotype Columbus by
Strathmore Publishing Services, London N7.

Printed and bound in Great Britain by
Mackays of Chatham PLC, Chatham, Kent.

Hodder and Stoughton Ltd,
A division of Hodder Headline PLC,
338 Euston Road, London NW1 3BH

CONTENTS

SERIES INTRODUCTION

The first task of philosophers is to ask questions – the questions which lurk in all our minds, but which, out of fear or confusion, we fail to articulate. Thus philosophers disturb us. The second task of philosophers is to try and answer the questions they have asked. But since their answers are inevitably only partial, philosophers both interest and infuriate us. Their third and most important task is to stimulate and inspire us to ask questions and seek answers for ourselves.

The human psyche or spirit has always been the main – although not the only – focus of philosophy. And inevitably when the psyche is explored, the gap between religion and philosophy rapidly narrows. Indeed for philosophers in the more distant past there was no gap at all, since philosophy was an aspect of theology and even mysticism. Although religious institutions are now quite weak, questions of spiritual philosophy are being asked more keenly and urgently than ever.

This series is an invitation to readers, with no philosophical training whatever, to grapple with the great philosophers of the spirit. Most philosophy nowadays is served in the form of brief summaries, written by commentators. Each of these books contains an introduction to the life and ideas of the philosopher in question. But thereafter the reader encounters the philosopher's original words – translated into modern English. Usually the words are easy to follow; sometimes they are more difficult. They are never dull, always challenging, and frequently entertaining.

INTRODUCTION

In the Qur'an, the holy book of Islam, the pious believer is exhorted to 'remember Allah with unceasing remembrance, and extol his limitless glory from morning till evening'. As Islam pushed outwards from the Arabian desert, creating a vast empire stretching from Spain and North Africa in the west to the Indian sub-continent in the east, its more devout followers started to wonder whether Allah was being forgotten. Spiritual teachers began to appear, urging people to turn away from the accumulation of wealth and power, and devote themselves instead to the attainment of spiritual wisdom and holiness. In the words of one of the first of these teachers, people should 'detach themselves from things, and attach themselves to the Lord of things'.

This was the origin of Sufism, one of the most creative religious movements the world has seen – and of which the philosopher and poet Rumi became one of the leading exponents. Gradually a number of simple Sufi maxims spread across the Islamic world, which were taken as defining the movement. 'Sufism is to possess nothing and to be possessed by nothing,' went one of these maxims; 'Sufism means being at ease with Allah,' went another; 'Sufism is keeping the heart pure from discord, and filling it with the love of concord,' went a third. All the maxims stressed in different ways that Sufism was primarily concerned with inner spiritual change, rather than outward religious observance. And very soon mystical literature of great beauty and depth began to appear.

The word 'sufi' refers to the coarse woollen garment which those committed to the Sufi way were given to wear. It was usually dyed blue, the colour of mourning, to symbolise that the Sufi was dead to material attachments and ambitions. Unlike Christian ascetics, Sufis were not required to be celibate, nor to withdraw from the world; on the contrary, most were married with children, and earned their living in normal occupations. They marked themselves out by putting themselves under a spiritual teacher who had attained a high degree of inner enlightenment, and following that teacher's instructions with unquestioning obedience. These teachers were thus at the heart of the Sufi movement, and many purported to trace their spiritual ancestry, from one teacher back to the one before, to Muhammed himself. The honorific title 'shaykh', meaning 'elder', was usually given to a teacher; and one who was especially wise was known as 'wali Allah', meaning 'friend of Allah' – referring to a verse in the Qur'an which states that 'the friends of Allah are free from fear and sadness', and a second verse, that 'Allah is a friend of those who trust him, taking them from darkness into light'.

Once accepted by a spiritual teacher, Sufis had to follow a path which took them through a succession of inner states. The first was repentance, in which the mind turns away from its former wants and pleasures, and makes spiritual enlightenment its overriding aim and purpose. This need not involve any practical changes in behaviour that are visible to observers; repentance and conversion involve an inner transformation of attitude. The second state is trust: in the words of one teacher, trust requires the individual 'to abandon every refuge except Allah'. This is followed by acceptance, in which the individual learns to regard all events and occurrences, even those that appear to be adverse, as ordained by Allah; and acceptance leads to gratitude, in which the individual gives thanks to Allah, even for the most extreme pain and suffering. The individual is now capable of truly selfless love, since all personal desires and needs have been eliminated. And love develops into inner intoxication, in which the spirit experiences a constant and unshakeable sense of joy.

Originally Sufism had no formal organisation or network; particular men and women were recognised as possessing great spiritual wisdom, and hence attracted followers. But gradually Sufi brotherhoods emerged, which authorised certain people to become spiritual teachers, and hence assured potential followers that these teachers would lead them on the authentic Sufi path. These brotherhoods also built lodges, where followers could listen to their teacher in relative comfort and tranquility. The lodges typically also provided free food and shelter for travellers and for the poor, and in some cases had small infirmaries where the sick could be nursed and treated. The Sufi lodges were probably established in Persia about three centuries after Muhammed's death; and they proved so successful in attracting new Sufi adherents that within a century Sufi lodges had sprung up throughout the Islamic world.

The first seven or eight centuries of Islam (from roughly the seventh to the fifteenth centuries of the Christian era) produced literature of the highest quality in almost every discipline, from science and medicine to philosophy and law; and since Arabic was the language of the Qur'an, it was universally used for scholarly discourse. Within the sphere of spiritual writing and poetry the Sufis were predominant; and they used the vernacular of the country in which they lived. Amongst the greatest of these Sufi writers was the Persian master Jalal al-Din al-Rumi, who lived in the seventh century of the Islamic era, the thirteenth of the Christian era.

Rumi was born in Balkh, a town in the far north

of the modern country of Afghanistan, in the year 1207 of the Christian era (592 of the Islamic era). His mother belonged to the local royal family, and his father claimed direct descent from a long line of religious leaders. Although remote from the heartlands of Islam, Balkh was renowned for its schools of philosophy and law, which had produced many fine scholars; Rumi's father seems to have been in charge of one of these schools. But in 1219, when Rumi was twelve, Balkh was attacked and virtually destroyed by Genghis Khan's Mongol army. Most of the leading families were put to the sword; and it appears that Rumi's mother was killed. But he and his father escaped, and began a long journey which lasted for the remainder of Rumi's childhood years.

They went first to the city of Nishapur, which was soon to suffer the same fate as Balkh. There they met the famous poet and teacher Attar, who presented Rumi with a copy of his *Book of Secrets*, a long poem about the mystical life – from which in later years Rumi loved to quote. From there Rumi and his father continued to Baghdad, the ancient capital city of the Islamic empire, which had only a few more decades of glory before it too was destroyed by Mongol invaders. The two travellers spent only three days there; and it is said that both felt extremely uneasy in the city, regarding its flamboyant wealth as an affront to the primitive simplicity of the Islamic faith. They decided to make a pilgrimage to Mecca.

From Mecca they moved northwards through Syria into Armenia, where they settled for four years. Rumi was now aged eighteen, and his father arranged for him to marry the daughter of another fugitive from the Mongol hordes. He also resumed his old occupation of teacher; and his reputation gradually spread, so that eventually he was invited to become the official religious teacher at the royal court in Rum (whose modern name is Konya), from where the Seljuk sultan ruled Asia Minor. Both father and son immediately felt happy in the city, and concluded that their years of wandering were over. In fact they both spent the rest of their lives there; and it is by the name of this city that the son continues to be known.

Shortly after their arrival, they were joined by another religious teacher who had fled from Balkh called Burhan. Thus, while Rumi's father fulfilled his duties at the court, Burhan devoted himself to teaching Rumi. During almost a decade of intensive study, which involved trips to Damascus and Aleppo to listen to other teachers, Rumi became a master of philosophy and theology. In 1240 he adopted the traditional turban and gown of orthodox religious scholars, and became a teacher himself. At this stage there was no sign of originality in his lectures; people were impressed only by the sharpness of his mind and the depth of his learning.

But in 1244, at the age of thirty-seven, he experienced an emotional and spiritual upheaval which transformed him. In that year a wandering Sufi called Shams appeared in Rum. Shams immediately attracted attention by his wild demeanour and eccentric behaviour. Most of the respectable citizens of Rum shunned him, but Rumi was enthralled by him. He invited Shams to live in his house, and for over a year the two men were inseparable. Rumi gave up his teaching; and his students became so incensed, and so jealous of their master's attachment to this strange intruder, that they threatened to attack Shams and chase him out of the city. When Shams heard about the threat, he ran away to Damascus. But Rumi was so distraught at the loss of his friend that he sent his eldest son to fetch him back. By now many of the leading figures in Rum were suspicious of Shams' influence, and they looked for an excuse to arrest and imprison him. Shams fled a second time; and on this occasion he left no word of his destination, and never returned.

The people of Rum expected their distinguished scholar to resume his former activities; but Rumi was no longer capable of sound philosophical argument, and no longer subscribed to the arid doctrines of orthodox theology. The sober lecturer had become the ecstatic mystic. Songs expressing his passionate love for God poured from his lips; and he frequently whirled and skipped in a frenzied dance to express his joy. His students were appalled at the change, and deserted him in favour of other teachers. But soon he attracted other disciples, whom he formed into a new Sufi brotherhood called the Mevlevis. Rumi developed a series of dances to be performed at their meetings, and the brotherhood soon became known as the Whirling Dervishes.

Poets were not held in respect in the Islamic world at this period; and Rumi himself, prior to his conversion, had spoken contemptuously of poetry, fearing that any form of free expression can easily lead people into heresy. But now he could not prevent himself from composing mystical verses, as the most potent means of conveying his spiritual experiences to others. He also told parables, to teach moral and spiritual truths in a way that would capture people's imagination. He was no longer content to confine himself to aspiring scholars, but wanted to reach out to anyone desiring a closer relationship with God.

His poetry and his parables were brought together after his death by his son, in a single vast tome called the *Masnavi*. Hailed by a later poet as 'the Qur'an of the Persian tongue', it takes the form of 25,000 rhyming couplets. A western scholar, R. A. Nicholson, who devoted a major part of his life to its translation, has said that it 'resembles a trackless ocean' in which there are no signs indicating different forms of expression or different themes; readers are compelled to find their own way through it. The poems are mostly spiritual explorations, in which through a mixture of images, paradoxes and syllogisms, readers are drawn into the inner world of Rumi's mystical vision. The parables are usually quite simple stories, sometimes with a twist, followed by an explanation, in which a moral is drawn or the characters are given symbolic significance.

Rumi made no attempt to place his thoughts and ideas into a coherent system; yet careful study of the *Masnavi* reveals a remarkable consistency, and one can even ascribe to Rumi a mystical philosophy. He makes a sharp distinction between the outer form of an object or creature, and the inner spirit; he regards the outer form as a veil, which the mystic learns to pierce. Indeed the purpose of treading the mystical path, Rumi declares, is to develop our powers of awareness, so that we can discern the divine spirit throughout creation. This leads him to explore the relationship of such awareness with the intellect. He regards the universe as the product of God's intellect, and thus believes that we can become aware of God in the universe if we subsume our intellect into his. Yet paradoxically this requires us to give up trying to acquire intellectual knowledge for ourselves, and to allow divine light to penetrate our mind; this enables us to know directly the inner truth of what the five senses perceive.

An accusation frequently made of Sufis is that they were so concerned with their own spiritual state that they were indifferent to moral and political matters. Rumi, however, was adamant that people could only make spiritual progress if they were virtuous in their behaviour, and that the visible fruit of inner enlightenment is a passion for justice. The root of moral evil, he believed, was not greed, lust or any of the obvious vices, but pride – the ego's desire to have power over other people. Rumi was critical of the tendency in Islamic thought to stress individual destiny, at the expense of moral freedom; he asserted that the individual has complete freedom to choose between good and evil, and thereby determine the course of life. Yet, paradoxically, he also says that the mystic should learn to accept all events, even apparently adverse ones, as manifestations of God's will – and thence find goodness and joy in every event.

Rumi does not question the orthodox doctrine that at death good people will be sent to paradise and bad people will go to hell – and that to some degree individuals are rewarded and punished while still on earth. Yet, like many mystics in both the Christian and the Islamic traditions, he finds it difficult to envisage God actually consigning people to eternal torment. To overcome this inconsistency he conceives God as possessing two opposing characteristics, mercy and anger, which are in constant tension – but generally mercy wins. This duality within God is matched by a similar duality within human beings – between love and hate – and love, in most people, ultimately proves stronger. Yet there is a crucial difference between God and humans in this regard: whereas God does not need to show mercy, since he is entirely self-sufficient, human beings can only find happiness and serenity if love dominates their lives.

Shortly after Rumi's conversion to mysticism the old king, who had originally invited Rumi and his father to the city, died, leaving three sons. Initially they fought amongst themselves for the succession, but eventually the middle son was victorious. He in turn appointed a chief minister, who was a firm admirer of Rumi. Thus Rumi and his Mevlevi brotherhood enjoyed protection. During the remaining three decades of Rumi's life, the brotherhood steadily grew and spread across Asia Minor and beyond. Thus by the time of his death in 1273 Rumi enjoyed the kind of fame and adoration that Francis of Assisi had attained a few decades earlier in western Europe. And, like the Franciscan order, the Mevlevi brotherhood continued to expand during the following centuries – and flourishes to this day.

In this present collection of Rumi's writings, pieces have been taken from the *Masnavi* which exemplify the main strands of his thought. Inevitably the different strands cannot be entirely separated from one another, so some of the pieces could readily have been put in more than one chapter. Nevertheless this process reveals an intellectual coherence which is not immediately obvious in the original text. As the chapter headings suggest, Rumi's mind relished paradox, and it is through resolving paradoxes that his mind moved forwards. The final chapter, containing a selection of his parables, may seem a little trite if read in isolation – as would the parables of Jesus Christ. Yet, as a later disciple of Rumi pronounced, every word uttered by the master must be understood at several levels – so his parables are intended to stick in the mind, and to reveal their meaning layer by layer.

ROBERT VAN DE WEYER

INNER AND OUTER

There are two worlds. There is the outer world which appears to exist, and seems solid and permanent, but in truth is an illusion. And there is the inner world which many people deny, and is invisible to the senses, and yet is real and eternal.

– I 795

The outward form passes away, but the world of meaning remains forever. How long will you be besotted with the shape of the jug? Look inside for the water. How long will you stare at the shell? Look inside, and pick out the pearl.

– II 1020–22

That which has no form creates form. That which has no existence brings things into existence. That which is hidden makes things appear. Form, existence, appearance – these are like dust carried on the wind, like the skin of an animal. That which does no work make the universe work.

– II 1280–22

Birds fly above and around us every hour of every day, and we barely notice them. But if one flies crookedly, it captures our attention. Those things which are outwardly peculiar are most liable to stimulate our senses, so that we seek the inner meaning.

– III 526

Wolves and dogs are distinct and separate types of animal; but the inner spirits of both are the same. The courtyards of different houses receive their own light from above; but the source and nature of the light is the same for all. Each person is distinct and separate, receiving particular guidance from God; but the inner spirit in all is the same, and the source of guidance is identical.

– IV 414–18

Externally the earth is made of dust. But internally it consists of light – the light which comes from God. The external is at war with the internal – as if the shell were at war with the pearl it contains. The external says: 'I am this and no more.' The internal says: 'Look closely, and you will find me.' The external says: 'The internal is an illusion.' The internal says: 'Just wait, and I shall reveal myself.'

- IV 1007–10

Ignore the outward forms of things. Do not concern yourself with the names people give to things. The form of a thing is a gate; the name of a thing is a title inscribed on the gate. Pass through the gate into the meaning within.

– IV 1285

The unbeliever argues: 'I can perceive nothing apart from what my five senses perceive.' But the unbeliever never reflects that the perceptions of the senses give news of that which is beyond their perception; they pick up hints of hidden wisdom. Indeed the purpose of the five senses is to induce the individual to seek this hidden wisdom.

– IV 2878-80

God has made the outer worlds appear real; and he has made the inner worlds seem unreal. But these are disguises, since the opposite is true. In the same way he has hidden the sea, but made the foam visible; and he has hidden the wind, but made the dust visible.

– V 1026–7

The form of an object is like a veil. Not every eye is capable of seeing through the veil. Those eyes that can penetrate the veil perceive divine craftsmanship. Your task is to develop your powers of perception so that you can tear aside every veil. When you succeed in this, you will realise that exertion and ambition are useless – that success and failure attach to the veil of things, not to their inner meaning.

– V 1551–4

Does anyone write on a page already covered with writing? Does anyone plant a sapling in a woodland already filled with trees? Look for the page which is blank, for the land where nothing has been sown. There you will find God; for God is most real where external reality is least evident.

– V 1960–63

How could the waves move and make foam without wind? How could dust rise from the dry earth without wind? Yet we cannot see the wind; we only infer it from its external forms. From every external form we can infer the divine spirit, the wind of God.

– VI 1459–60

SPIRIT AND BODY

We think of ourselves in terms of the different parts which comprise the body. But, like the sun, we are one substance. In the shadow of ignorance the head and the foot seem quite different. In the pure light of truth they are one.

$$- \text{ I } 686\text{--}8$$

Holy people polish their breasts until every mark of greed and malice, dishonesty and hatred, has been cleaned away. Then their hearts can be mirrors on which images of infinite beauty are reflected. Eventually on the mirror of the heart the form of the one who is formless, the image of the one who is invisible, will appear. This form, this image, cannot be contained within heaven; it cannot be encompassed by the largest palace; it cannot be supported by the foundations which hold up the earth. All these things have limits; but the divine form and image has no limit. Is it not wonderful that a holy heart can reflect it? Faced with this miracle, the intellect must remain silent.

$$- \text{ I } 3484\text{--}9$$

Once your heart becomes pure and clear, it will become a mirror on which pictures will appear from beyond the realm of earth and water. Not only will such pictures appear, but also the image of the one who painted them.

– II 72–3

Where there is pain, the cure will come; where the land is low, water will flow. If you want the water of mercy, go low. Go down deeply into the world of the spirit, and you will find it. Drink deeply from it, and you will become intoxicated.

– II 1939–40

The body is visible, the spirit hidden. The body is like the sleeve, and the spirit is like the arm within the sleeve. The intellect is also hidden. The senses connect the body and the outside world with the intellect and the spirit. You see someone move, so you know there is life; but you do not know from outside observation that this life contains intellect and spirit.

– II 3253–5

Experience shows that the spirit is nothing but awareness. Those who have greater awareness have greater spirits. The human spirit is greater than the animal spirit, because it has greater awareness. The angel spirit is greater than the human spirit because it has greater awareness. The spirit of a saint is greater than the spirit of a novice because it has greater awareness. Those who have less awareness should make themselves subject to those who have greater awareness. A rose does not bow down to a thorn; the thorn is below the rose.

— II 3326–32

A lover seeks his beloved; but he also wants his beloved to seek him. God seeks every human being, but he also wants human beings to seek him. A lover feels flashes of lightening in the heart – flashes of joy – and wants to know that his beloved feels the same. God takes joy in humanity, and wants to know that humanity takes joy in him. Have you ever heard one hand clapping? God is one hand; humanity is the other.

— III 4393–9

If you beat a porcupine with a stick, it becomes large and fat. The more you beat it, the more it thrives. The human spirit is like a porcupine. The more it is beaten by the blows of suffering, the larger and more healthy it becomes. That is why God inflicts especially heavy blows on those whom he wishes to make into prophets.

– IV 97–100

The body moves by means of the spirit, but you do not see the spirit. Thus you can know the spirit through the movement of the body.

– IV 155

Your body, with its various qualities and abilities, is merely borrowed. You do not possess it, but have it on loan for a period. So do not set your heart on the body. Your spirit by contrast is yours forever. Rejoice in its qualities and abilities, and nurture them, for they are more precious than heaven itself.

– IV 1840–41

God wants us to live according to the spirit he has planted, expressing the inner spirit in words and actions. By expressing our own inner spirit, we are making manifest the hidden spirit of God. In this way we fulfil God's purpose for us on earth.

– V 246–7

The body frequently oppresses and torments the spirit. The spirit is a falcon, but the body is a crow. Falcons receive many wounds from crows.

– V 842–3

The spirit does not depend on the life of the body. The spirit is like the head of a bird; the heart is the wings; the body is the feet. The spirit can fly on the wings of the heart, without need of feet.

– V 1721

Hunger is the king of food; when we are hungry, we demand nourishment. In the same way, hunger of the spirit is the king of religion. Hunger makes even quite unpleasant food seem pleasant. In the same way hunger of the soul enables us to endure considerable suffering in the service of God.

– V 2832–5

CREATION AND DESTRUCTION

The divine father has given names to every creature on earth. He never forgets how he fashioned every creature, so he understands every creature perfectly. He will care for every creature until the end of time. He is wonderfully nimble in coming to the aid of creatures in distress; he is never slow. Amongst human beings, he made some to believe in him and know him, and he made others to remain ignorant of him.

– I 1234–7

If inner meanings were all that mattered, God would not have bothered to create the world. If loving God were purely a spiritual state requiring no outward expression, God would not have bothered to create the world. Just as lovers show their love through material tokens, God expresses his love through creation – and we must express our love for him by the way we use his creation.

– I 2624–7

The beauty and splendour of God belong to him; the beauty and splendour of his creatures are borrowed from him.

– II 1103

All people can see the handiwork of God; it is all around them. Few can see the attributes of God which brought that handiwork into existence.

– II 2812

The fruits of God's mercy are manifest everywhere. But who knows and understands the essence of God's mercy? Few can know the essence of his mercy, or of any of his other attributes, except through their effects and by analogy.

– III 3635–7

Those who deny God often say: 'If the spirit of God were present in Nature, we would be able to see it.' But if a child cannot see the intellect within an adult, does that mean the intellect does not exist? If a rational person is insensitive to the movements of love, does that mean that love is an illusion?

– III 4796–7

Remember that you are unique. Your beauty is special; no one on the earth looks exactly like you. God knows you for what you are – since he created you.

– IV 806–7

God created us in his own image. To describe God is to describe perfect humanity.

– IV 1194

God did not become greater by bringing the universe into existence; he did not change from his former state. But the exercise of his power became greater. Thus we must distinguish between God himself and the exercise of his power. It is through his power that God becomes manifest to us, and this is the proof of his existence.

– IV 1666–9

God created the universe in order to manifest himself – in order that the treasure of his wisdom may not remain hidden. He reveals to us the immeasurable wealth of his truth. In the same way we manifest spirits by our actions; let our actions be true to our spirits.

– IV 3028–9

The realm of creation has different categories of creature, each with different qualities and aims. The Creator has no categories, and no purpose which can be defined. So when God gives commands, do not look for a purpose in those commands; there is none. On careful inspection it appears that the human intellect and spirit have no purpose, and cannot be divided into categories; within the spirit there is no separation and no joining. This is because the intellect and spirit derive directly from God, and remain connected to him.

– IV 3692–6

God has already honoured every human being, setting a royal crown on every head, and a garland around every neck. Human beings are the kings and queens of his creation; and he has made earth and heaven to be their palaces. Human beings sit on a high throne; other creatures are on the steps leading up to the throne.

– V 3574–5

God's love is the sun of perfection; his commands are light shining from the sun; the creatures on earth are his shadows.

– VI 983

God can both create and destroy; you can exalt and abase. Without these opposites God could not act. Look at the land: half the year it is abased, and nothing grows; during the other half it is exalted, yielding every kind of crop. Look at your body: sometimes it is abased through illness; sometimes it glows with health. Think of every form of abasement in the world: famine and drought, warfare and poverty. They abase us, in order that we can be exalted.

– VI 1847–52

Think of all creatures as pure and clear water, reflecting the attributes of God. Every creature possesses something of the knowledge, justice and kindness of God; they are like stars in the night sky reflected in flowing water. A good king reflects the power of God. A good scholar reflects the knowledge of God. Generations come and go, and each generation is a new generation, reflecting the divine attributes in a new way. Yet the attributes themselves do not change; justice is the same justice, and knowledge the same knowledge. People and nations may change as one generation replaces its predecessor; but the inner meanings are constant and eternal. The water flowing in the stream changes many times every hour; but the moon and stars reflecting in its water stay the same.

– VI 3172–8

TRUTH AND FALSEHOOD

We know the sun exists, but we can never see and understand it because our eyes cannot bear to look directly at it. The intellect knows that love exists, but it cannot understand love because it is incapable of looking directly at it. The sun alone explains the sun; love alone can explain love.

— I 115–16

Sometimes God shows us the way to go; sometimes he shows us the opposite way. The work of religion is full of bewilderment. But it is not a bewilderment that turns us away from God; it is a bewilderment that leads us to drink from his love, and become utterly intoxicated.

— I 311–13

The bodily senses are the windows through which we can see the outward signs of God. Yet the windows are distorted, and the pure light of God's truth becomes divided into different and diverse colours.

— II 186–7

The pillar of this world is blindness to the truth; awareness of the truth would destroy the great edifice of human vanity, and lay it flat. Awareness is like the sun, and blindness like ice; awareness is like water, and blindness like dirt. Awareness can melt blindness; it can wash away the scales that prevent human beings from perceiving the truth.

— I 2066–9

Just as genuine and counterfeit currency can circulate simultaneously, so truth and falsehood can co-exist. Those who are unable to distinguish truth from falsehood are living in darkness. They are like travellers in the night, not knowing in which direction they are going. The task of religious teachers is to enable people to see what is true and what is false. A jeweller needs to learn to tell the true ruby from a worthless stone; a merchant must learn to tell genuine currency from forgeries. To become holy a seeker must learn to tell divine truth from worldly falsehood. And as a person grows in holiness, night turns into day.

— II 285–93

Those who take pride in their knowledge enjoy an audience, so they can show off their expertise. For them knowledge is not desired for its own sake, but as a bait with which to draw people into their circle of admirers. But this kind of knowledge is worldly, and does not bring spiritual freedom.

– II 2427–31

If you desire to become spiritually rich, make yourself poor in worldly knowledge. Such knowledge is concerned with your lower nature; and, seen from the perspective of true knowledge, it is a fantasy. The acquisition of worldly knowledge may increase your status in the eyes of others; but spiritual knowledge carries you up higher than the heavens.

– II 3201–3

You need to acquire knowledge whose roots lie deep within the realm of meaning. Every branch leads back to its roots. You need knowledge whose wings will carry you across the ocean of form to the continent of meaning.

– III 24–5

The philosopher, relying on books and ideas, is a prisoner of what he has learnt. The sage, who receives his knowledge from God, is set free. Knowledge from God is the kernel, while knowledge from books is the husk. The stomachs of animals prefer the husks, while humans thrive on the kernels.

– III 2527–8

There are people whose heads are filled with knowledge of worldly matters, who are familiar with all the sciences, and yet do not know their own spirit. They know about everything except themselves. They do not know whether or not they are in harmony with God. They know the precise value of every object they buy and sell; but they do not know their own value. They look up at the sky, and can distinguish auspicious stars from inauspicious ones; but they do not know whether they will rise to life after death. To know yourself, and thence to know your relationship with God, is to be a master of the highest science.

– III 2648–54

To be unable to perceive the essence of God's attributes is the fate of most people, but not of everyone. God's attributes are mysteries; the essences of these attributes are mysteries of mysteries. Those who attain holiness are able to penetrate these mysteries of mysteries, and so understand the essence of God himself. They become true lovers of God, and God does not conceal anything from them.

– III 3650–53

If you want to see truth, close your eyes to what appears to be true. See that the things which seem most real are actually least real. See that the ideas which exercise the greatest fascination for the intellect are actually the least interesting. Until now you have been like a beggar, pleading for some gift that does not exist. You have been like a merchant, seeking profit in a business that can only make a loss. You have been like a farmer ploughing a barren field. You have been like a student in a school where the teachers know nothing. You have been slave to a master who does not exist. Look instead for the divine treasure-house that to naked eyes is invisible.

– VI 1360–67

You take great pride in your own intelligence; you are filled with the wind of your own cleverness. Yet if your spirit is to be healthy, you must become a simpleton – not a simpleton warped by buffoonery, but a simpleton distracted and bewildered by God. God gave you your intelligence in the first place; now sacrifice it at the altar of God. Truly intelligent people happily put their intelligence on the altar; only those who combine cleverness with folly are reluctant. If your intellect departs from your head, your hair will be a divine crown.

– IV 1402-8

Knowledge acquired through learning, and knowledge as a gift from God, are as different and as far apart as earth from heaven. Knowledge from God is like the light of the sun; knowledge through learning is merely the dull reflection of that light. Knowledge from God is like a raging fire; knowledge through learning is like a spark from that fire.

– V 459–61

You are not a prophet, so you cannot work out entirely for yourself how you should think and behave. Yet you are free to choose whether or not to follow the way that the true prophets have shown. You are like dough; with the yeast of prophetic teaching you shall rise.

– V 1051–2

Pride is concern for your own skin. It is an obsession with how you appear to others. Your pride forces you constantly to think about your position in society, and the style of the property in which you live. So what is pride? Pride is lack of concern for what lies beneath the skin. Pride is blindness to the light which illuminates the heart.

– V 1933–7

God's intellect created the universe, and causes the stars to move across the sky in perfect harmony. Your intellect comes from his. But if you try to use it alone, without reference to his, it will become a barrier between you and him. Allow your intellect to be subsumed into his; only use your intellect in obedience to God's will – for accomplishing the tasks which he sets.

– V 3233–6

SIMILARITIES AND OPPOSITES

God created suffering and heartache so that joy and happiness could clearly be seen and appreciated. He hid many truths so that people would seek them; and when they had discovered them, they would rejoice in them to the full. God hid himself so that people would have to strive hard to find him – and only then would they understand him for what he is. Yet God is unique. We know joy by its opposite, suffering; we know light by its opposite, darkness. But God has no opposite; either we perceive him with the eyes of the spirit, or we are spiritually blind.

– I 1130–36

The task of life is to bring harmony between opposites. Strife between opposites is destructive; harmony between opposites is creative. God wants the sheep and the lion to live in peace.

– I 1293–4

Look at those two partners washing clothes. Outwardly they seem to be in conflict. The first puts the clothes in the water; the second takes them out, and squeezes them dry; the first throws them back in the water – only for the second to take them out again to squeeze. Yet in fact they are working in harmony. The first applies soap; the second squeezes out the soapy water; the first rinses; the second prepares them to be hung out on the line. Opposites may seem to be in conflict; but in truth opposites depend on one another.

– I 3082–6

The light of faith opposes the fire of sensuality. The light of faith causes justice and generosity; the fire of sensuality causes greed and anger. Yet before letting the light of faith shine on the fire, quench the flames of the fire with the waters of mercy. The waters of mercy – the sense of divine forgiveness – enable the green plants of virtues to spring up around the dying embers. When the fire is no longer blazing, the light of faith will shine more brightly. And the green plants will create a beautiful scene.

– II 1250–54

What do empty people find attractive? Empty lies.
What do stupid people find attractive? Stupid ideas.
Each finds its own kind attractive. No cow ever felt
attracted towards a lion.

— II 2055–6

Those who devote themselves to competing with
others, seeing others as rivals for wealth and position,
do not understand themselves. They feel themselves
to be too similar to others; thus they need to assert
their distinctiveness by rising above others.

— IV 803–4

You cannot recognise evil as evil until you have experienced goodness. You discern something through its
opposite.

— IV 1345

A bird who has never tasted pure water, drinks and
washes its wings in a salty pond. A person who has
never been caressed regards violence as normal.

— V 597–9

LIFE AND DEATH

———◆———

The death of the body is like the breaking of pomegranates. The sweet and juicy pomegranates go into the pot; but those that are dry and bitter are cast aside. Yet before the pomegranates are broken they all look the same.

— I 707–9

Before I was born, waiting in the womb, I felt terribly afraid; I thought that birth would be death, since it would force me to leave my familiar surroundings. Then at my birth I realised that my fears were unjustified. Far from being death, birth was release from prison, into a world of bright colours and sweet smells.

— I 791–2

Every day God is at work; he is never without action and activity. Amongst his daily acts, he sends out three armies. The first army goes to pregnant mothers, to ensure that their children grow in their wombs. The second army goes to the places where mothers are giving birth, to ensure that the world is filled with both male and female. And the third army goes to the people who are dying, to give them a spirit of gratitude for all they have received on earth, and hope for the future.

– I 3071–5

For a human being to be brought into existence a spirit must come down from heaven and enter the womb of a pregnant woman, giving life to her unborn child. For a spirit to make this journey it must be humble, and it must possess great courage. After death the spirit returns to heaven.

– III 460–64

Death has the same colour as life. Those who live as God's enemies die as God's enemies. Those who live as God's friends die as God's friends. A mirror put in front of a beautiful person shows beauty; a mirror put in front of an ugly person shows ugliness. If you fear death, it is because you fear yourself. It is your own spiritual ugliness that truly frightens you, not death itself. The good person will die a good death; the bad person will die a bad death.

– III 3439–43

When your ship capsizes and you are thrown into the water, you are liable to sink so long as you remain alive. But once you have died, your corpse will rise to the surface.

– III 3460

The mother suffers great pain in childbirth. To the baby childbirth is release from prison. The mother weeps with joy when the baby is born. The baby screams, as if to say: 'Deliverance has come; I am free.'

– III 3560–61

Physical birth is release from the prison of the womb into the freedom of the world. Spiritual birth is release from the prison of the senses into the freedom of God.

– III 3574–6

Long ago I died to the life of a speck of dust, and became a plant. Then I died to the life of a plant, and became an animal. Then I died to the life of an animal, and became a human being. Next I shall die to the life of a human being, and spread my wings to rise up amongst the angels.

– III 3901–3

God brought you to birth, conferring upon you his attributes; eventually you will return to him. You came down from the sky through the clouds; eventually you will rise up through the clouds to the sky.

– III 4165–6

The water of life cannot be seen; it can only be tasted. Let religious teachers guide you to the stream where it flows. Then lower your jug into it, and wait until it becomes heavy.

– III 4302–6

From time to time disease enters the body. It causes damage by tearing apart the four elements within the body. The four elements are like four birds with their feet tied together; illness and disease untie the feet. The four elements are like four branches of a tree; illness and disease pull the branches from the trunk. The pain which accompanies illness is caused by this tearing and pulling within the body. The religious healer, guided by God, seeks to tie the bird's feet back together; he grafts the branches back on the trunk. Yet he cannot always succeed, since God has appointed for each of us a time of death, when the elements will finally separate, and the body will dissolve.

– III 4426–32

Why should it be surprising that a human spirit cannot remember where it came from – where it resided before it was born. To enter the world is to be shrouded by a veil, so the spirit can no longer see its former abode, which is heaven. The task of the human spirit on earth is to make the veil transparent, so the spirit can gaze clearly at heaven. The veil is the body; so to make the veil transparent means purifying the body of all moral stains.

– IV 3632–6

Human beings on earth have evolved. They started as no more than specks of dust. Then for a period they lived amongst the plants; and at that stage they remembered nothing about their former existence in the dust. Then for a period they lived amongst the animals, forgetting their former state among plants. Then they became fully human, forgetting their former state among animals. Yet, although we forget our past as a species, we are still affected by it. We feel great sympathy and concern for the earth, for plants and for animals; without knowing the cause, we still regard them as friends.

– IV 3637–40

It was God, our creator, who guided us through the stages of evolution, making us into full human beings. His purpose was to make us intelligent and aware, so that we might know him. He also wished to give us the strength of will to free ourselves from base and selfish desires.

– IV 3646–9

To die in the sure hope of union with God is a sweet prospect. But to live in the knowledge of being separated from God would be intolerable bitterness.

– V 4117

THOUGHT AND FEELING

How wide is the ocean of the intellect! How broad is the knowledge which the intellect can encompass! In the sweet ocean of the intellect all manner of ships and boats are moving this way and that. When they are filled with knowledge, they sink into the ocean; and then the knowledge is understood.

– I 1109–12

Let me discover the place in my spirit where speech develops without words. In this place the spirit is able to express the glory of God. In this place words are replaced by images. But they are not physical images; they are images of that which does not physically exist. In this place imagination breaks the boundaries of existence, reaching outwards to infinity. Imagination transcends the limitations of the five senses, rising upwards to that realm which has no horizon – the realm where all is one, and one is all.

– I 3092–9

The fire of sensuality is the source of sin and error. Physical fire can be quenched with water. The fire of sensuality can only be extinguished by religion. The light of God puts out the blaze of bodily desire.

– I 3697–9

Intellectual knowledge about religious matters is the bane of the spirit. Such knowledge is like borrowed money; it does not belong to the person who possesses it. Yet those who amass intellectual knowledge about religion believe that they are acquiring religion itself. You must become ignorant about religion; you must become ignorant about worldly matters too. In fact you must become completely mad. Whatever may be profitable to you, flee from it. Whatever may advance your interests, shun it. If anyone presses you, curse them. Lend money to those who have no hope of returning it. Be indifferent to physical danger, and walk freely through places that others avoid. Throw away your reputation, and be free of shame. When you have done all this, you will have acquired true knowledge.

– II 2326–34

The house of the heart which has no windows facing the divine sun is dark and miserable. It feels cramped and dirty, cold and damp. In fact it is like a tomb.

– II 3129–31

The intellect is luminous, and seeks that which is good. The ego is dark, and seeks that which is evil. So how can the dark ego vanquish the luminous spirit? The home of the ego is the body, and the body treats the intellect as a stranger.

– III 2557–8

God created the angels, and put within them intellect. He created animals and put within them sensuality. He created human beings and put within them both intellect and sensuality. Those human beings in whom intellect dominates sensuality are higher than angels. Those human beings in whom sensuality dominates intellect are lower than animals.

– IV 1496–7

The intellect has two ways of operating. The first way is acquired; it is learned from books and teachers, by reflection and rote, through concepts and their application. The more the intellect learns in this fashion, the heavier it becomes, weighing down the spirit. The second way is a gift, bestowed by God. This gift comes from the spirit into the intellect, like a fountain shedding water. When the water of divine knowledge bubbles up from the spirit into the intellect, it is fresh and sparkling; it never becomes stagnant or dull.

– IV 1960–63

Presiding over his court a magistrate seems very important; but when the king comes, the magistrate slips off into a corner. Intellect is like the magistrate; it dominates human activity. But when God comes, intellect is utterly insignificant. Intellect is a shadow, and God is the sun; when the sun shines directly, shadows disappear.

– IV 2110–11

Without doubt the intellect and the heart are directly linked with God. But most intellects and most hearts are veiled from his light.

– V 619

GOOD AND EVIL

If you want to know the form of the ego, read about hell and its seven gates.

– I 779

The human ego is a part of hell. All parts of an entity possess the nature of the whole.

– I 1375

A clever man denies the existence of the devil. At that moment the devil seizes him. Have you never seen the devil? Look at your face in the mirror. Can you not see the traces of the devil?

– I 3283–5

Malice is a plant whose roots lie in hell. The enemy of malice is religion.

– II 274

Look at the jars in the pharmacy. The pharmacist has carefully placed each substance in a separate jar. Occasionally the contents are spilt, so that two substances are accidentally mixed. The pharmacist then carefully unmixes them, grain by grain, putting each grain back in its proper jar. In the same way good and evil are quite different; but in this world they have been spilt and mixed. The task of the religious teacher is to separate good from evil – or, rather, to demonstrate to others how they can separate them.

– II 280–84

The ego is like a thief, trying to steal and destroy the spirit. Do not concern yourself with the ego's concerns; reject the ego. Concern yourself only with the concerns of God.

– II 1063

We cannot deny that God is responsible for evil, just as he is responsible for good. Yet this does not diminish his generosity. His bestowing evil is part of his perfection. Here is an example. A painter creates two kinds of picture, beautiful and ugly. He can portray delightful young maidens; and equally he can portray nasty criminals. Both kinds of pictures display his mastery. The ugly pictures do not reflect his ugliness, but rather his creativity. In his creative genius he can reveal the full horror of ugliness, and thus reveal the perfection of his artistry. If he were not able to paint ugly pictures, he would be imperfect. That is why God has created both selfish unbelievers and honest believers. In this respect both faith and unbelief bear witness to him; both through their behaviour pay homage to his power. The difference is that the unbeliever does not recognise this, and pursues other aims; while the faithful believer rejoices in serving God.

– II 2535-45

Since good and evil are mixed together in this world, the same events may simultaneously express God's promises and his threats. Since truth and falsehood are mixed together in this world, God reveals himself and hides himself in the same events.

– II 2965–7

When someone insults or criticises you, a small ant of hatred is born in your heart. If you do not squash that ant at once, it quickly grows into a serpent, and then into a dragon.

– II 3466–7

There is no absolute evil in the world, since evil is relative. One person's freedom is another person's shackle. One person's food is another person's poison. For the snake, poison is life, but for humans it is death. The fish needs water to breathe, while humans drown in water.

– IV 65–9

Hell is a factory which makes anger and malice. Those who purchase the goods of this factory cut themselves off from religion, and become incapable of showing mercy.

– IV 111–12

Human beings are made from clay; but do they resemble clay? Does a grape resemble the vine from which it comes? Does theft have the same shape as the gallows? The origin of something is not the same as the object itself; an action is not the same as its consequence. Yet the origin gives rise to the object; an action gives rise to its consequence. Remember this when you choose between good and evil. Goodness may at times be painful, but its consequences are joyful. The opposite applies to evil.

– V 3978–88

You should regard every day as a day of justice, in which you give people their due. After all, every morning you give your feet their due, by putting shoes on them; and you give your head its due by putting a hat on it.

– VI 1887

What is justice? To order some matter correctly. What is injustice? To order some matter incorrectly.

– VI 2596

Nothing that God has created is vain. No human behaviour is wholly wrong, be it anger or patience, innocence or guile. Nothing is absolutely evil or absolutely good. The benefit and harm of everything depends on the situation. For this reason wisdom is vital and knowledge useful.

– VI 2597–9

Hell is a dragon with seven heads. Greed is the bait which draws you there.

– VI 4657

Let me distinguish between compulsion and free will by describing movements of the hand. When you are frightened, your hand trembles; that movement is involuntary. But if you decide to move your hand away from danger, you are acting freely. Both actions are ordained by God; but morally they are quite different. You may repent of having moved your hand, if later you think you were wrong. But only a fool would repent of a trembling hand.

– I 1496–9

The first thoughts are the last to be realised. We conceive our purposes first, and then we conceive the means of fulfilling them. But in actuality the means come first, and the purposes are the consequences. Initially you conceive a tall tree in your garden; then you consider where best to obtain a sapling. But planting the sapling occurs many years before you possess a tall tree in your garden. Long ago God conceived a glorious, harmonious universe, and then considered how to create it. He planted the universe; but it has not yet realised its purpose.

– II 970–74

The sun, moon and stars move across the sky involuntarily; so their movement deserves neither reward nor punishment. The whole world glorifies God; but that glorification was ordained by God, and so also deserves no reward. Only actions undertaken freely will be judged on the day of reckoning. Free will is the salt of religion.

– III 3287–90

Actions do not have the same colour as the reward or retribution they will incur. No service has the same colour as the payment received for it; nor does the labourer's work resemble his wage. The reward or retribution for your actions will match the inner meaning of those actions, not their outward form.

– III 3445–6

Look at the stars in the night sky. The astrologers tell us that the movements of these stars sustain and guide the world. But they do not affect the realm of inner meaning – the realm of the spirit. Think of a tree. The branches bear the fruit; but it is the inner energy of the tree that makes the fruit grow and gives it life. Inner meaning gives purpose to existence; it is because the gardener wants the fruit that he plants the tree and tends it.

– IV 519–24

The thief tries to deny that he has stolen, but the judge forces him to confess. The gifts we enjoy come from God. Let us not be thieves by pretending to possess them for ourselves. God is our judge; he knows the truth, and will eventually confront us with our crime.

— IV 1014–16

When God assigns a particular lot to a person, this does not preclude consent, desire and freedom. God sends suffering to all of us from time to time. Some react by fleeing from God; others react by moving closer to him. In battle all are in danger of death. The cowards freely choose to retreat; the brave attack the enemy with even greater vigour. Suffering and fear are sent by God to everyone; and each person freely decides how to respond.

— IV 2914–20

The world is like a courtroom, with God as judge. We are called to act in such a way that the judge finds us innocent, explaining to him each of our actions in terms of the laws he has decreed. Yet so often we act without thinking; or we act well, but do not bother to explain ourselves to the judge.

— V 174–6

No one says to a stone, 'You have come late,' or to a stick, 'Stop beating me.' Nor do we say such things to a person under compulsion, or even to a person who has an excuse. Commands, prohibitions, wrath, honour, rebuke – these things concern only those who possess free will.

– V 2967–73

The angel and the devil, displaying their wares, make our freedom real. Free will is a faculty within us; when we see the differing objects of desire, we can exercise that faculty.

– V 3004–5

God's free will has given rise to our free will. His free will is invisible beneath the dust; ours is visible. His free will creates our free will. When he gives a command, he does not compel obedience, but invites it.

– V 3087–8

From time to time heartache ambushes you, attacking your sense of joy. Do not worry: it is preparing you for deeper happiness. Heartache sweeps away the false joys that had obsessed you, and compels you to seek solace in the only true source of joy – God himself. It shakes the yellow leaves from your spiritual tree, so fresh green leaves can grow in their place. It pulls up the old roots of happiness, so that new roots can push downwards, deep into the soil of ecstasy. Heartache extracts many things from the heart, so that far better things can take their place.

– V 3678–83

Your actions on earth continue to cling to you, like a child clings to its mother's skirts.

– VI 419

If no one were ambitious for status and power, where would evil find soil in which to grow? Those in whom the poisonous fruits of evil thrive provide food for the dogs of hell. But if there were no ambition, there would be no conflict between people, and hence no cause for anger and hatred. How can ambition be destroyed? Only mercy possesses the weapons to kill ambition; only mercy can replace conflict with gentleness.

– IV 1075–9

When you look carefully, you see that the world is caught up in war. Nation is set against nation in the pursuit of power and wealth. Belief is set against unbelief in seeking the hearts and minds of the common people. Animal is set against animal in the struggle to survive.

– VI 36–8

To understand the conflict within God's creation, look at the four elements. The four elements are like four sturdy pillars holding up the roof of heaven. Yet each pillar tries to destroy another – such as water, which puts out fire. So creation is built on opposites; and these inevitably are at war.

– VI 47–50

The world is equally full of joy and suffering. Without union there could be no parting and separation; the existence of harmony presupposes the possibility of conflict. Why is there such opposition? Why does divine unity give birth to this multiplicity? The reason is that the four elements are the roots of creation, and the creatures of the earth are the branches. The roots determine the nature of the branches. Yet the spirit is not caught up in this opposition, this multiplicity. The spirit shares the qualities of the divine unity.

– VI 60–63

The cruelty of events, the bitterness of every kind of misfortune, are easier to bear than being distant from God. Cruelty and bitterness will pass; but distance from God may last for eternity. No one enjoys continuous good fortune; but closeness to God is an eternal blessing.

– VI 1756–7

God's mercy is greater than his wrath. So instead of fearing his wrath, seek his mercy.

– IV 3205

Everyone is aware of God's gentleness, and everyone is aware of his severity. Everyone flees from his severity, and clings to his gentleness. But God has hidden severity within his gentleness, and hidden gentleness within his severity. This is God's subtlety, his guile. In this way people of discernment, who see the light of God, may be separated from those who see only the surface of things.

– V 419–20

Which will prove victorious, mercy or anger? Which will triumph, the pure springs of Paradise or the raging fires of Hell? Some people live by anger – angrily asserting themselves over others, and provoking God's anger. Others live by mercy – showing mercy to others, and receiving God's mercy. God invites each of us to choose mercy or anger.

– V 2123–5

When we speak of the fires of hell, we are using an image for God's anger. Yet although he has the power to punish us, his cool gentleness is far greater than his hot wrath. Coolness always precedes hotness; so enjoy his gentleness, and give him no reason to become angry.

– IV 3742–4

God's anger is truly terrifying. But once you begin to tremble, and thus acknowledge your fear, then his anger subsides. While you ignore his anger, you stand in danger of punishment. But when you bow down to his power, his anger turns into gentleness and kindness.

– IV 3753–4

LOVE AND NEED

When you are a lover, you want your beloved to be a lover also. God is humanity's greatest lover; and we, his beloved, must become his lovers.

– I 1736

The thirsty seek water. But water also seeks the thirsty.

– I 1741

An action may be coated in sugar. But if it is not prompted by love, it causes great bitterness of spirit – both for the perpetrator and the victims. What is meant by bitterness of spirit? It is to advance towards bodily death without drinking the water of life.

– I 3686–7

True beauty is not merely a matter of outward form; it is also a matter of inward spirit. Someone who appears beautiful, but whose spirit is ugly, is a living lie. In choosing a partner ensure that the inward spirit is truly beautiful – because outward beauty will soon tarnish and decay.

– II 703–5

Desire for God leads us to want to know God. Knowledge of God causes us to love him. It is impossible to love God if you have a false conception of him. But those who possess true knowledge of God cannot help loving him.

– II 1532–4

The creed of love transcends the specific creeds of the different religions. We do not need to define true religion by statements of belief. We need only say that we are lovers of God.

– II 1770

Everyone was made for a particular task. God has put in every heart desire for that task, and satisfaction in undertaking it. How would the hand and the foot ever move, unless prompted by desire? How would a stick or a leaf move across the ground without wind?

– III 1618–19

All of us love that which is beautiful; and beauty is defined as that which we love. A wood-carver tries to turn a lump of wood into a beautiful object, in order that he may love it. But it is far better to love another human being than something inanimate. You may be tempted to choose someone cold and unloving, in the hope that little will be demanded of you; but you will find that getting love out of such a person is like extracting money from a money-lender. Do not look for someone to replace your mother or father; intimacy with a mother's breast is quite different from intimacy with a lover's breast. Choose as your partner someone who shines on you, whose brightness illuminates the darkest corners of your heart. Yet before you make your choice, be careful. Ensure that the beauty is real, and not counterfeit – like a lead coin coated in gold plate. The right partner is someone whose external beauty is exactly matched by internal virtue.

– III 545–55

Where there is illness, cures will come. Where there is poverty, wealth will follow. Where there are questions, answers will be given. Where there are ships, water will flow. Spend less time seeking water, and more time acquiring thirst. Then water will gush forth from the ground.

– III 3210–12

In his wisdom God has ordained and decreed that people should love one another. He has ordained in particular that male and female should cherish one another. Throughout the natural order he has put the male and female into pairs, and implanted in each desire for the other. He has also ordained that heaven and earth should be in love; earth is like a magnet, and heaven like iron.

– III 4400–403

The female desires the male, and the male desires the female, that each may perfect and complete the other, and that the human race may continue through their union. Thus sexual desire is holy and good.

– III 4414–16

When a candle flickers in darkness, the moth flies into the flame and is consumed. The candle of God flickers in the darkness of the world; let us fly towards the flame, and be consumed by God's love.

– IV 3801–5

In comparison with love for God, every other kind of love is idle infatuation. Love for God is that flame, which when it blazes, burns away everything except God. Love for God is a sword which cuts down all that does not belong to God. God alone is eternal; all else will vanish. God alone is the true object of desire; all other objects are idols which should be burnt or cut to pieces.

– V 586–90

Love cannot be contained within our speaking and listening. It is an ocean whose depths cannot be plumbed. Would you try to count the drops of the sea? Love is greater than that number.

– V 2731–2

Each human being, each animal and each plant is beautiful, if that creature is living as God ordained. Thus we can worship God by loving all that is beautiful.

– VI 3753–4

My religion is love. I want all the physical movements of my body to be motivated by love, and my spirit to be overwhelmed by love. In so far as my body and spirit are not permeated by love, I am ashamed.

– VI 4059

The blind can only find the path if they are guided by people with eyes. In the same way the spiritually blind can only find their path to God if they are guided by people with religious vision. The blind do not sow, reap, build or trade; they depend on others to provide what they need. Yet those who are capable of sowing and reaping, building and trading, are not self-reliant either; they depend on God to bless and make good their efforts. The blind carry a cane to prevent then stumbling. Faith is the cane on which every person depends; without it we are all liable to stumble.

– I 2125–6

God cries out to humanity, 'Come quickly, I am a giver, in need of receivers. I have bounty, and I need beggars.' God is like a beautiful woman in search of an undistorted mirror, so she can enjoy her beauty. God wants to enjoy his generosity.

– I 2744–6

Purify yourself from the attributes of self, and you will find the purity of your true self.

– I 3466

Go to the workshop where the universe was made, and see the Worker. But in order to reach the workshop, you must first understand that the universe is a veil. Thus the Worker requires you to penetrate the veil, if you are to meet him face to face. When you enter the workshop, you will understand why the veil was created.

– II 759–62

Kill the cow of your ego as quickly as you can, so your spirit can come to life and attain true knowledge.

– II 1446

If you want to sit with God, go first and sit with those who know God. If you ignore people of holiness, you will be lost. But remember the devil wants you to be lost, so he will constantly try to persuade you that the company of holy people is dull and profitless.

– II 2163–5

The suffering in this world is terrible. By comparison the suffering needed to prepare yourself for the next world is trivial. Happy are those who accept the suffering required in pursuit of spiritual perfection. The pointless suffering of the world brings no reward; but religious suffering brings an eternal reward.

– II 2472–4

People often say they do not have time to practise religion; so they ask religious people to pray on their behalf. But when they make this request, they have no passion; they say the words as if they were mumbling in their sleep. Their excuse for failing to practise religion is that all their time is devoted to feeding their families; and they say this is their primary duty. So they escape from God, and devote themselves to food; they escape from religion, and make food their idol. They love the world and its bounty; but they happily ignore its Creator. They relish luxury and comfort; but turn their backs on the source of this generosity.

– II 3067–75

Prophets and religious teachers are like signs on the road, to guide spiritual travellers. But those who have encountered God directly no longer need signs. Their inner eye, combined with the divine lamp, is sufficient to keep them on the right path. Such people then become signs for others.

– II 3312–14

Whether seekers run or walk, eventually they will find what they are seeking. So devote yourself to seeking God. And to make your search easier, first find someone to guide you on the path.

– III 978–9

Do not concern yourself with whether you are ugly or beautiful; concentrate on the beauty of the One whom you are seeking. Do not concern yourself with whether you are weak or strong, vile or pure; concentrate on the strength and purity of the One to whom you aspire. Even if you are more beautiful, strong and pure than anyone else in the world, your beauty, strength and purity falls far short of God's. Think of yourself as someone with parched lips, looking for water. Your dry lips bear witness to your need – and hence bear witness to God.

– III 1437–42

To become holy, you must die to self, and live for the Lord. Only then are the mysteries of God constantly on your lips. To die to self requires great self-discipline, in which you endure great physical and emotional pain.

– III 3364–5

When a candle is burning on a bright day, the flame of the candle is so overwhelmed by the sun that it is barely visible. The flame does not cease to exist; but its light is wholly absorbed into the sunshine. In the same way, when a person's spirit comes near to God, it is overwhelmed by the spirit of God. The individual spirit continues to exist; but its love is wholly absorbed into God's love.

– III 3669–73

When you have a direct encounter with God, do not look to the sciences to assure you that your encounter is genuine. In fact, once you have perceived the beauty of God, the sciences lose their fascination. Vision is greater than knowledge, since vision is personal, whereas knowledge is based on hearsay. But most people are not interested in attaining vision. Knowledge of the sciences is like ready cash, which can give immediate benefits in the world. The effort required to attain spiritual vision is like paying a debt owed to the next world. – III 3856–9

To grow close to God is to escape from the prison of our present existence. To grow close to God is to cease feeling happy or unhappy; it is to leave the realm where you can be early or late; it is to transcend the distinction between fact and falsehood.

— III 4514–16

You are a lover of God. When God comes to you, not a single hair on your head will remain. At God's glance you, and a hundred like you, will be annihilated. In loving God, you are allowing your own self to be destroyed. In the presence of God you will be reduced to a mere shadow.

— III 4621–3

Once you have encountered God directly, you have no more need for hearsay. Hearsay is for those who are absent from God, not those who are present. To encounter God directly is like meeting your lover; you have no more need for go-betweens carrying messages. Before encountering God, you rely totally on religious teachers, and must trust their words. But after encountering God, you receive knowledge from its source.

— IV 2066–70

People often describe the process of growing closer to God as climbing a spiritual ladder. This may seem to be an apt metaphor. But only when you stumble and fall off the ladder, plunging into the depths below, do you truly come close to God.

– IV 2763–5

God implants in our spirits desire; and the focus of that divine desire is God. – IV 2909

You are like a person who has a basket of bread on his head, yet goes from door to door asking for food. Look to yourself, not to others, for the spiritual nourishment you need. You are like a person up to his waist in water, begging others to give him drink. Look to yourself to slake your spiritual thirst.

– V 1073–5

Those who are beginning on the religious path are like infants. Just as infants think only of milk and sweet foods, so religious beginners are concerned only with pleasant spiritual experiences. When infants start to walk they are very proud of this achievement; but they frequently fall over. In the same way religious people start to engage in theological argument, feeling very pleased with their proficiency; but they frequently trip.

– V 1287–91

God has planted within you the desire to search for him. Do not look at your lack of strength and wisdom for the search. By planting within you the desire to search, God is guaranteeing the strength and wisdom you need. Also he is telling you that you are worthy of him.

– V 1733–5

The sense of self is like an intoxicating wine. It removes intellect from the head and modesty from the heart. The sense of self is like a deadly enemy that lies in wait, and springs countless ambushes, destroying our best intentions.

– V 1920–21

One day a woman asked her lover, 'Do you love me more than you love yourself?' He replied, 'I love you so much that I am full of you from head to toe. There is no distinction between loving you and loving myself; loving myself is loving you.' If you love God, you will feel towards him as that lover felt towards his beloved.

– V 2020–24

If you try to destroy your ego when you lack the spiritual knowledge to succeed, you are like a brigand with a rusty sword. Just as a rusty sword is liable to break, enabling the victim to escape, so your ego will survive. In fact your ego will be more cunning and wily in the future, and will be more difficult to slay. Ensure that your sword is strong before you attack the ego.

— V 2821–5

I cannot bear the thought that God might depart from me, and leave me alone. He can inflict any pain and suffering upon me that he wants, so long as he stays close to me. A hundred thousand deaths, each in the most appalling agony, are better than separation from God.

— V 4114–15

As we travel closer to God, we begin to desire him. We can feel his attraction drawing us onwards. This attraction is proof of his existence. Does dust rise up without a wind? Does a ship float without the sea?

— V 4216–17

If you had sufficient imagination, you would realise that your present existence is illusory; and you would feel terrified. You are like a lover who has fallen in love with a paper doll; if the paper doll were to disintegrate, the lover would be terrified at his own folly.

– VI 1447–9

God is profoundly and overwhelmingly attractive. But do not wait to feel that attraction; exert yourself now. You are a spiritual warrior; so regardless of how you feel, you must exert yourself in the cause of truth. Do not concern yourself with whether you desire God or not; simply act as if you do.

– VI 1477–80

God enters the spirit. He takes away anger and puts contentment in its place. He takes away stinginess, and puts generosity in its place. Morning and evening these transactions occur.

– VI 3332–4

A single brick of grace is more precious than a thousand bricks of obedience. The devil can easily remove the bricks of obedience. But a brick of grace can never be shaken.

– VI 3869–70

PARABLES

The Shopkeeper and the Parrot

There was once a shopkeeper who owned a green parrot. The parrot had a fine voice and was extremely talkative. He perched on a bench outside the shop and made conversation with all the customers.

One day the parrot sprang off the bench and flew away, spilling the bottles of rose-oil as it went. Eventually the parrot returned. But the shopkeeper was so cross at the spilt rose-oil that he struck the parrot on the head with his hand. Immediately the parrot's head went completely bald – and it stopped talking.

The shopkeeper was distraught. 'With my parrot bald and silent,' he wailed, 'all pleasure has gone out of my life. What a fool I was to strike the poor bird.' He begged all the priests and holy men in the district to come and cure his parrot. But all were defeated.

Eventually a traveller from a distant city called at the shop. This man was completely bald. He sat down on the bench where the parrot was perched, and did not utter a word. The parrot stared at the man.

After several minutes the parrot could restrain

himself no longer. 'Why are you completely bald, and why do you keep silent?' the parrot asked, 'Did you spill bottles of rose-oil?'

The shopkeeper was overjoyed to hear his parrot speak again. And the people standing by laughed at the parrot comparing himself with the traveller.

The moral is: do not judge others by your own standards.

The Scholar and the Boatman

A great scholar, who was an expert in grammar, embarked on a boat. As the boat crossed the wide river, the scholar turned to the boatman, with a self-satisfied smirk on his face. 'Have you ever studied grammar?' the scholar asked. 'No,' replied the boatman. 'Then half your life has gone to waste,' the scholar pronounced.

The boatman felt very sad at the scholar's judgement. Presently a storm blew up, and the river turned into a mass of violent whirlpools. 'Have you ever learnt how to swim?' the boatman asked. 'No,' replied the scholar. 'Then the whole of your life has gone to waste – the boat is sinking in these whirlpools.'

The moral is: scholarship by itself only makes a person proud; it must be complemented by practical skill.

The Deaf Man and the Sick Neighbour

A deaf man heard that one of his neighbours was ill. He felt he had a duty to visit his sick neighbour, to give comfort. But since he would not be able to hear his neighbour's words, he would have to guess what he said – and respond accordingly. He thought carefully in advance what his sick neighbour was likely to say, and prepared his replies. Then he went to the neighbour's house.

'How are you?' the deaf man asked. 'Dying,' the neighbour replied. 'Thank God for that,' the deaf man said.

'What have you been drinking?' the deaf man asked. 'I think I drank poison, put into my cup by an enemy,' the neighbour replied. 'I am delighted to hear it.'

'Which doctor has been attending you?' the deaf man persisted. 'The Angel of Death – now get out!' the sick man shouted. 'Thank God you are receiving such skilful care,' the deaf man replied. 'Now I must be on my way.'

'This man is my enemy till breath leaves my body,' the sick neighbour thought as the deaf man left.

The moral is: a sense of duty is not enough; wisdom to know when to act, and when to do nothing, is equally important.

The Man and his Thornbush

A man planted a thornbush on the edge of his land, near a busy road along which many people walked each day. As the months and years passed, the thornbush grew bigger, dropping its thorns on the road. The feet of the poor who could not afford shoes were lacerated by the thorns, leaving a trail of blood on the road nearby.

People begged the man to root up the thornbush. But he always replied that he would wait until tomorrow to do so – and tomorrow never came. Finally the thornbush grew so large that the king himself came, and urged the man to tear it up.

The man looked at the huge bush, and began to weep. 'Your majesty,' he replied, 'the bush is now so large that I am not strong enough to tear it up.' So the king ordered his soldiers to do the job; and he threw the man in a dark dungeon.

To interpret the story, note: the thornbush represents human sin; the king and his soldiers represent God and his angels.

The House with No Roof

A man decided he needed a larger house for himself and his family. He offered his present house for sale, and immediately someone came and purchased it. So he was in a great hurry to buy another house. He asked a friend to help him find one.

The friend took him to a large, old house on the edge of the town. The roof had collapsed and the walls were crumbling. 'If only this house had a good roof and sound walls,' the friend said, 'it would be perfect for you and your family.'

The man was furious. 'You idiot,' he shouted, 'you're just wasting my time.'

The moral is: do not live by 'ifs' but by truths.

The Wall and the Pond

A rich man had a pond near the edge of his garden, and the garden was surrounded by a high wall.

One day a traveller passed by, desperate with thirst. He climbed up the high wall and looked over. When he saw the pond, he longed to drink from its clear water. But the wall was so high that he did not dare jump down. And the stones on the far side were so smooth that he could not climb down.

So one by one he took the stones from the wall and threw them into the pond. The sound of the stones splashing into the water was beautiful to his ears. As the wall got lower, the pond rose higher. Eventually he was at the same level as the water and could drink from it.

To interpret the story, note: the rich man represents God; the traveller represents any human being; the pond is the water of life; and pulling down the wall that divides us from the water of life, is prayer.

The Man with Double Blindness

A blind man stood by the road, crying out, 'Have pity on me. I am doubly blind. So show me double compassion.'

People said to him, 'We can see that you are blind in your eyes, but what is this second blindness?'

'I have an ugly voice with an unpleasing tone,' the man replied. 'Thus when I cry out, people are so offended that they turn away. As a result, I cannot look at them, and they refuse to look at me – I am doubly blind.'

As people heard these sad words, their hearts filled with compassion. And their compassion transformed the sound of the blind man's voice in their ears: it no longer seemed ugly, but sounded soft and sweet. This prompted them to give generously to him.

The moral is: if we are warm and compassionate towards one another, we shall regard one another as beautiful – and we shall be generous and unselfish in our behaviour.

The Horse That Could Not Drink

Every morning a man took his horse to the village pond to drink the water. As soon as they arrived at the pond, the man would coax the horse. 'Come on,' the man would shout, 'drink up. You need water to survive – the sun will be hot when you are pulling the plough. Drink up, I say.'

The man meant well. But the horse could not drink while the man was watching him and coaxing him. He felt so self-conscious and anxious that his throat refused to swallow. He put his mouth to the water trying to drink; so the man thought his horse was responding to his coaxes. In fact the horse did not take a drop.

This persisted day after day. And each day the horse became more and more dehydrated. As the man saw his horse wasting away, he became more and more worried, and coaxed the horse even more volubly. But this only made the horse more anxious, and his throat even tighter. Eventually the horse died.

The moral is: busybodies, who are constantly telling others how they should behave, frequently do more harm than good.

The Elephant in the Barn

The people of a particular town had never seen an elephant. One night, when everyone was asleep, a group of travelling showmen brought an elephant into the town. The showmen never displayed this elephant publicly in a market-place, because this would enable people to see it without paying. Instead they put it in a darkened building, and charged people to go in. So in this particular town they hired a barn; and the next day people flocked to feel this strange creature.

Some who came into the darkened barn felt the trunk, and were convinced the creature was the shape of a water-spout. Some felt the ear, and believed the creature was the shape of a fan. Some felt a leg, and believed it was the shape of a pillar. Some felt the back, and believed it was the shape of a throne.

Soon the entire town was engulfed in furious arguments, as people debated the shape of the animal.

The moral is: each of us is blind to the whole truth, and at best we can sense only one part; so we should never imagine we possess the whole truth, and never fall out with those who perceive different aspects.

The Huge Snake

A snake-catcher, who made money by displaying exotic snakes in the market-place at Baghdad, went into the mountains in search of more of these vicious reptiles. High in the mountains, where snow had fallen, he came across a vast snake that appeared to be dead. It was so huge that it would take several men to lift. And he reckoned that if he could get it to Baghdad it would cause quite a stir.

So he went and fetched some friends, and together they hauled it to the city. Great crowds gathered to catch a glimpse of the huge snake. Many declared that it was not a snake, but a dragon.

But because it seemed to be dead, no one was frightened.

However, as the warm sun unfroze the body of the huge snake, it began to stir. Then it slowly uncoiled itself. The snake-catcher and the onlookers could hardly believe their eyes, and for a few moments did not move. With a sudden jerk the snake lifted its head, and began to attack the crowd.

People turned and ran. Several were crushed to death in the stampede, and many were badly injured. The snake finally turned on the snake-catcher himself, and killed him.

To interpret this story, note: the large snake represents our sinful desires; never become complacent about sin, believing that it is dead.

The Lost Camel and the Reward

A man owned a large number of camels. One day his favourite camel went astray. The man was distraught at losing such a fine creature. So he offered a substantial reward to anyone who could tell him where his camel was.

Dozens of people came to see him, telling him where his camel might be. None of them knew, but each hoped that if his guess were correct, he would receive the reward. The owner responded eagerly to every suggestion. He never found the camel, but he became so exhausted that he died.

The moral is: do not trust people who are motivated by material reward; they will destroy you.

The Physician and the Lunatic

A distinguished physician asked his pupils to administer a particular drug to him. 'But that drug is for lunacy,' said the pupils, 'and your mind is so powerful that it could never go mad.'

'A lunatic came up to me today,' the physician replied, 'and turned his face to me. He smiled and winked at me, and tugged at my sleeve. If he had not recognised me as similar to him, he would not have been so friendly towards me.'

The moral is: we should take note of how others see us; they may understand us better than we understand ourselves.

The Moon and the Eyebrow

Two men were looking up at the night sky. 'Look at the new moon,' the first one said. 'The moon hasn't risen yet,' the second replied. 'Besides, the new moon is not due for several days.'

The first man remained convinced that he could see a new moon. The second man went over to a nearby pond, and scooped up some water in his hands. He wet the first man's eyebrows, which were very bushy, and brushed them upwards.

'Can you still see a new moon?' the second man

asked. The first man looked up, and to his astonishment found that the narrow crescent had disappeared. 'You were merely seeing a loose hair from your eyebrow,' the second man said.

The moral is: be careful that what you think you see and know is actually true.

FURTHER READING

The only complete translation of Rumi's *Masnavi* was made by R. A. Nicholson in eight volumes, with a detailed commentary.

A. J. Arberry has translated many of the parables, in *Tales from the Masnavi*, published by Curzon Press.

William C. Chittick has produced a guided anthology in *The Sufi Path of Love*, published by the State University of New York Press.